MY LIFE JOURNAL

NAME ___________________________

____

WWW.DAILYTRANSFORMATION.ORG

Who Benefits

THERE ARE FOUR GROUPS THAT OFTEN FEEL HELPED BY THIS JOURNAL

- **Seekers:** This is one who wonders if God has a name, knows their name and cares about them. People are meeting God and being transformed by Him.

- **Scattered Sheep:** These are folks who are growing in their relationship with God, but don't know where to worship. Many are finding the journal helps "church themselves" in this season.

- **Stuck Sheep:** Others love their place of worship but feel like their walk with God is stalled. People are getting unstuck practicing these habits.

- **Shepherds:** Those who care for God's sheep need ongoing nourishment in their own walk with God. This journal is helping shepherds cultivate not only a first love relationship with Jesus but also a renewal of bearing first things fruit (Revelation 2:1-7).

As you think about those you love, consider where they are on their journey. Imagine… practicing the habits with them and growing together. Where will you start? On the next page learn about the four habits and which page you can find its tutorial.

HOW *My Life Journal* CAN HELP YOU PRACTICE
4 THINGS SO YOU WILL THRIVE WITH JESUS:

LISTEN: *"I will guide you along the best pathway for your life..."* **Psalm 32:8 NLT**

God is speaking and He wants to walk daily with you to accomplish His work through you. This journal has a section for you to write down prayer requests and promptings from God so you can keep bringing these concerns to Him. .... ***(begins on page 3***

INQUIRE: *"If you look for Me in earnest, you will find Me when you seek Me."* **Jeremiah 29:13 NLT**

Read your Bible each day to meet with God and inquire of Him. God wants us to seek Him with all our hearts, and when we do, He meets with us. In the next section we provide help that many have found allows them to search for Jesus and His direction as they read through the Bible.. ***(begins on page 9***

FELLOWSHIP: *"And let us consider how to stir up one another to love and good works, not neglecting to meet together, as is the habit of some, but encouraging one another, and all the more as you see the Day drawing near."* **Hebrews 10:24-25 ESV**

When we seek Jesus as our God and Leader, we discover He has given us a family. He is the Father and His other followers are our siblings. God will not only personally encourage us as we face struggles, He will use His family. Find or gather a group of people wanting to learn about following Jesus. Together you can read and study the Bible. You can even share a meal. We have included instruction and *Weekly Fellowship Meeting pages* to record what you learn as you gather. ....***(begins on page 117***

eXPRESS: *"For you are a chosen people... This is so you can show others the goodness of God, for He called you out of the darkness into His wonderful light."* **1 Peter 2:9 NLT**

God desires us to include others in His family. Sharing the love of God through care and the truth of Jesus will help people make the most important choice of life. We have included help for expressing your story and a place to write down the names of those with whom you are sharing Jesus' love.
....***(begins on page 136***

LISTEN

LISTENING: Learning To Pray

• • • • • • • • • • • • • • • • • •

God desires that we have a thriving relationship with Him through healthy communication. Prayer is talking with God. It certainly includes asking Him to help us and those
in our lives. But, healthy communication includes listening. The Holy Spirit wants to
guide you in how to pray. He will add people to your prayer list and provide leadership
in how to follow Him. Remember, you face Spiritual battle every day. Satan wants to
defeat you through temptation and fear. Prayer can strengthen you for every situation
that you have yet to encounter this day.

If you wonder how to pray, you are not alone. Those closest to Jesus asked for
help. Jesus taught them in Matthew 6:5-8 to be honest (v5), humble (v6) and real
(v7-8). Then He gives 6 things to pray for:

Praise of God: *"Our Father in heaven, hallowed be Your name,"* (V9)

Commit to His **Purposes**: *"…Your kingdom come, Your will be done, on earth as it is in heaven."* (V10)

Ask for **your Needs**: *"Give us today our daily bread."* (V11)

Ask God for **Forgiveness**: *"And forgive us our debts,"* (V12)

Pray for **Others**: *"as we also have forgiven our debtors.* (V12, 1 Timothy 2:1)

Ask for **Protection**: *"And lead us not into temptation, but deliver us from the evil one."* (V13)

Scan and watch video for additional help

Exercise: Ask God to show you how to pray for each of these six areas and note on
the "Prayers & Answers" page. For instance, *"God, show me Your qualities so I may
praise You. Lord, what is Your will for…? What are my needs?"*

Remember the encouragement Jesus taught through the Apostles:

- John wrote…*"…the Spirit who lives in you is greater than the spirit who lives in the world."* 1 John 4:4 NLT

- The Apostle Paul: *"Be glad for all God is planning for you. Be patient in trouble, and always be prayerful."* Romans 12:12 NLT

- James, Jesus' half-brother wrote: *"You do not have…because you don't ask God!"* James 4:2 NLT

- Peter and John prayed: *"…enable your servants to speak your word with great boldness. Stretch out your hand to heal and perform signs and won-ders through the name of your holy servant Jesus."* Acts 4:29-30 NIV

Note the Prayer/Answers pages that follow. Through your day, listen to the Holy
Spirit's prompting to pray for people. It may come in silence in your Quiet Time with
God or as you see a person in your day. If you sense a leading, step out and offer to
pray with that person. List the prayer concerns and the date God answers. We encourage you to carry the journal with you so you can add/update throughout your day.

PRAYERS & ANSWERS

DATE	PRAYER	ANSWERED

DATE	PRAYER	ANSWERED

PRAYERS & ANSWERS

DATE	PRAYER	ANSWERED

PRAYERS & ANSWERS

DATE	PRAYER	ANSWERED

INQUIRE

INQUIRING: GET ACQUAINTED WITH DAILY READING & JOURNALING

Our motivation for reading the Bible is not only to get instruction for life each day, but also because God wants us to truly know Him. Reading the Bible is time with God. Look for Him. Listen to His Spirit as you read your Bible. Jesus prayed, *"And this is eternal life, that they know you the only true God, and Jesus Christ whom you have sent."* John 17:3 (ESV). The word "know" in this verse is a word for marital intimacy. You can *know* God intimately!

As you journal, at times, what God gives you will also benefit someone else. Below is a great way to not only record, but also quickly find what God says to you each day.

Table of Contents
Look over your journal. You'll notice that near the front there are 4 pages which will become your Table of Contents. This will be filled in each day by you after you do your journal entry.

Daily Journal Pages
The Daily Pages will be where you will make your entries as you follow the Bible reading program found at the end of your Daily Journal Pages. You will need to number these pages individually.

Bible Reading Program
Following a reading program is important for accountability, discipline and for systematic instruction in God's Word. As you mark off each day of the reading plan in this journal, you will read through the Old Testament once in a year and the New Testament twice. A reading plan helps you avoid a common pitfall of reading your favorite six books again and again. As a result you'll be missing 90% of what he wants to say to you (for there are 66 books in the Bible).

HOW TO USE THE *Daily Reading* & JOURNALING PAGES

Step 1: Ask the Holy Spirit to teach you and reveal Jesus to you. Jesus said about His Spirit, *"When he comes, he will convict the world about sin, righteousness, and judgment"* John 16:8 CSB

Step 2: Read the Bible verses. As you are reading, underline anything the Lord impresses on you as a personal word to be applied. When you read with an open heart, the Lord will give you words of encouragement, direction and correction (2 Timothy 3:16).

Step 3: After you are finished with the daily reading, turn to a fresh page in your Daily Pages to record what God has shown you.

- Enter the date
- Title the page
- Write down a topic that generally describes what you have learned.
- Use the acrostic S.O.A.P. to record what God has shown you. (See example on page 12)

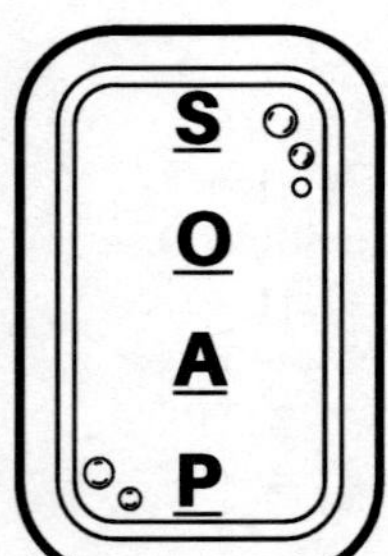

Scripture............Record the main Bible verse.

Observation....Record the circumstances you observed in the verses.

Application......Describe how you will be different today because of what you have just read.

Prayer.................Record a prayer of commitment and help applying what you learned.

(see sample on next page)

HOW TO USE THE *Daily Reading* & JOURNALING PAGES

• • • • • • • • • • • • •

4/23	"Hope to Share"	1
DATE	TITLE	PAGE

SCRIPTURE

Jesus – "What I tell you in the dark, say in the light, and what you hear whispered, proclaim on the housetops."
Matthew 10:27 (ESV)

OBSERVATION

This amazes me that the God of the universe wants to talk with us. But, it seems to be for a reason. We're supposed to share it. Jesus tells us not to be afraid of people. Fear God. God is like a Father and doesn't want any of us to be destroyed. So, don't fear people.

APPLICATION

Am I hearing God? If not, is it because I'm not spending time alone with Him? I must confess, I'm too busy. I need to rise when my home is quiet to spend time praying, listening to my loving Heavenly Father. Oh, may He give me a message that I can bless those around me. And, may He strengthen me to courageously keep communicating when someone dismisses what I share.

PRAYER

My Jesus, help me hear from You as I read your word and as I pray. I quiet myself and ask You to speak even though today feels like darkness. Give me Your light, that I might offer hope to my family and co-workers. In Jesus' Name I Pray, Amen.

How will I Be Different Today Because of What I Just Read?

HOW TO USE THE *DAILY READING* & JOURNALING PAGES

Step 4: Turn to the Table of Contents and catalog your entry by date, scripture, topic/Title and page.

Table OF CONTENTS

DATE	SCRIPTURE	TOPIC/TITLE	PAGE
4/23	Matthew 10:27	Hope to share	1
4/24	Psalm 109:21	God protects me from my enemies	2
4/25	1 Chronicles 10:13	Earthly consequences for my sin	3

Step 5: Conclude your daily devotional time by turning to the Prayer List and intercede for yourself and others.

REMEMBER! My Life Journal is designed to serve you in your growth with Jesus. You can be flexible in how you use it, but be sure to develop a healthy habit of spending time daily with the Lord.

Some ask, when is the best time for my quiet time devotion with God? The answer is: when you are at your best! If you are a morning person, do your quiet time then. If you are at your best in the afternoon, then spend time then to study the Word. The bottom line is: Jesus deserves your best, so give Him the best part of your day!

Scan and watch video for additional help

TABLE OF CONTENTS

DATE	SCRIPTURE	TOPIC/TITLE	PAGE

Table OF CONTENTS

. . . .

DATE	SCRIPTURE	TOPIC/TITLE	PAGE

TABLE OF CONTENTS

DATE	SCRIPTURE	TOPIC/TITLE	PAGE

TABLE OF CONTENTS

DATE	SCRIPTURE	TOPIC/TITLE	PAGE

Daily Journal Pages

· · · · · · · · · · · · · · · · · ·

How will I be different today because of what I just read?

How will I be different today because of what I just read?

DATE	TITLE	PAGE

How will I be different today because of what I just read?

How will I be different today because of what I just read?

<table>
<tr><th>DATE</th><th>TITLE</th><th>PAGE</th></tr>
</table>

How will I be different today because of what I just read?

How will I be different today because of what I just read?

DATE	TITLE	PAGE

How will I be different today because of what I just read?

How will I be different today because of what I just read?

How will I be different today because of what I just read?

How will I be different today because of what I just read?

How will I be different today because of what I just read?

<table>
<tr><th>DATE</th><th>TITLE</th><th>PAGE</th></tr>
</table>

How will I be different today because of what I just read?

How will I be different today because of what I just read?

How will I be different today because of what I just read?

<table>
<tr><td>DATE</td><td>TITLE</td><td>PAGE</td></tr>
</table>

How will I be different today because of what I just read?

<table>
<tr><th>DATE</th><th>TITLE</th><th>PAGE</th></tr>
</table>

How will I be different today because of what I just read?

How will I be different today because of what I just read?

<table>
<tr><td>DATE</td><td>TITLE</td><td>PAGE</td></tr>
</table>

How will I be different today because of what I just read?

How will I be different today because of what I just read?

<table>
<tr><td>DATE</td><td>TITLE</td><td>PAGE</td></tr>
</table>

How will I be different today because of what I just read?

DATE	TITLE	PAGE

How will I be different today because of what I just read?

How will I be different today because of what I just read?

DATETITLEPAGE

How will I be different today because of what I just read?

How will I be different today because of what I just read?

How will I be different today because of what I just read?

<table><tr><td>DATE</td><td>TITLE</td><td>PAGE</td></tr></table>

How will I be different today because of what I just read?

How will I be different today because of what I just read?

How will I be different today because of what I just read?

How will I be different today because of what I just read?

How will I be different today because of what I just read?

<table><tr><td>DATE</td><td>TITLE</td><td>PAGE</td></tr></table>

How will I be different today because of what I just read?

How will I be different today because of what I just read?

How will I be different today because of what I just read?

How will I be different today because of what I just read?

How will I be different today because of what I just read?

How will I be different today because of what I just read?

How will I be different today because of what I just read?

<table>
<tr><td>DATE</td><td>TITLE</td><td>PAGE</td></tr>
</table>

How will I be different today because of what I just read?

DATE	TITLE	PAGE

How will I be different today because of what I just read?

How will I be different today because of what I just read?

How will I be different today because of what I just read?

How will I be different today because of what I just read?

How will I be different today because of what I just read?

How will I be different today because of what I just read?

How will I be different today because of what I just read?

How will I be different today because of what I just read?

How will I be different today because of what I just read?

How will I be different today because of what I just read?

How will I be different today because of what I just read?

How will I be different today because of what I just read?

How will I be different today because of what I just read?

How will I be different today because of what I just read?

How will I be different today because of what I just read?

How will I be different today because of what I just read?

<table>
<tr><th>DATE</th><th>TITLE</th><th>PAGE</th></tr>
</table>

How will I be different today because of what I just read?

How will I be different today because of what I just read?

How will I be different today because of what I just read?

DATE	TITLE	PAGE

How will I be different today because of what I just read?

DATE	TITLE	PAGE

How will I be different today because of what I just read?

<table><tr><td>DATE</td><td>TITLE</td><td>PAGE</td></tr></table>

How will I be different today because of what I just read?

<table>
<tr><td>DATE</td><td>TITLE</td><td>PAGE</td></tr>
</table>

How will I be different today because of what I just read?

How will I be different today because of what I just read?

DATE	TITLE	PAGE

How will I be different today because of what I just read?

How will I be different today because of what I just read?

How will I be different today because of what I just read?

<table>
<tr><th>DATE</th><th>TITLE</th><th>PAGE</th></tr>
</table>

How will I be different today because of what I just read?

How will I be different today because of what I just read?

<table>
<tr><td>DATE</td><td>TITLE</td><td>PAGE</td></tr>
</table>

How will I be different today because of what I just read?

READ THROUGH THE BIBLE ①

JANUARY

1. ☐ Gen. 1,2; Luke 1
2. ☐ Gen. 3-5; Luke 2
3. ☐ Gen. 6-8; Luke 3
4. ☐ Gen. 9-11; Luke 4
5. ☐ Gen. 12-14; Luke 5
6. ☐ Gen. 15-17; Luke 6
7. ☐ Gen. 18,19; Ps. 3; Luke 7
8. ☐ Gen. 20-22; Luke 8
9. ☐ Gen. 23,24; Luke 9
10. ☐ Gen. 25,26; Ps. 6; Luke 10
11. ☐ Gen. 27,28; Ps. 4; Luke 11
12. ☐ Gen. 29,30; Luke 12
13. ☐ Gen. 31-33; Luke 13
14. ☐ Gen. 34-36; Luke 14
15. ☐ Gen. 37,38; Ps. 7; Luke 15
16. ☐ Gen. 39-41; Luke 16
17. ☐ Gen. 42,43; Ps. 5; Luke 17
18. ☐ Gen. 44-46; Luke 18
19. ☐ Gen. 47,48; Ps. 10; Luke 19
20. ☐ Gen. 49,50; Ps. 8; Luke 20
21. ☐ Ex. 1,2; Ps. 88; Luke 21
22. ☐ Ex. 3-5; Luke 22
23. ☐ Ex. 6-8; Luke 23
24. ☐ Ex. 9-11; Luke 24
25. ☐ Ex. 12,13; Ps. 21; Acts 1
26. ☐ Ex. 14-16; Acts 2
27. ☐ Ex. 17-20; Acts 3
28. ☐ Ex. 21,22; Ps. 12; Acts 4
29. ☐ Ex. 23,24; Ps. 14; Acts 5
30. ☐ Ex. 25-27; Acts 6
31. ☐ Ex. 28,29; Acts 7

FEBRUARY

1. ☐ Ex. 30-32; Acts 8
2. ☐ Ex. 33,34; Ps. 16; Acts 9
3. ☐ Ex. 35,36; Acts 10
4. ☐ Ex. 37,38; Ps. 19; Acts 11
5. ☐ Ex. 39,40; Ps. 15; Acts 12
6. ☐ Lev. 1-3; Acts 13
7. ☐ Lev. 4-6; Acts 14
8. ☐ Lev. 7-9; Acts 15
9. ☐ Lev. 10-12; Acts 16
10. ☐ Lev. 13,14; Acts 17
11. ☐ Lev. 15-17; Acts 18
12. ☐ Lev. 18,19; Ps. 13; Acts 19
13. ☐ Lev. 20-22; Acts 20
14. ☐ Lev. 23,24; Ps. 24; Acts 21
15. ☐ Lev. 25; Ps. 25,26; Acts 22

16. ☐ Lev. 26,27; Acts 23
17. ☐ Num. 1,2; Acts 24
18. ☐ Num. 3,4; Acts 25
19. ☐ Num. 5,6; Ps. 22; Acts 26
20. ☐ Num. 7; Ps. 23; Acts 27
21. ☐ Num. 8,9; Acts 28
22. ☐ Num. 10,11; Ps. 27; Mark 1
23. ☐ Num. 12,13; Ps. 90; Mark 2
24. ☐ Num. 14-16; Mark 3
25. ☐ Num. 17,18; Ps. 29; Mark 4
26. ☐ Num. 19,20; Ps. 28; Mark 5
27. ☐ Num. 21-23; Mark 6,7
28. ☐ Num. 24-27; 1 Cor. 13

MARCH

1. ☐ Num. 28,29; Mark 8
2. ☐ Num. 30,31; Mark 9
3. ☐ Num. 32,33; Mark 10
4. ☐ Num. 34-36; Mark 11
5. ☐ Deut. 1,2; Mark 12
6. ☐ Deut. 3,4; Ps. 36; Mark 13
7. ☐ Deut. 5,6; Ps. 43; Mark 14
8. ☐ Deut. 7-9; Mark 15
9. ☐ Deut. 10-12; Mark 16
10. ☐ Deut. 13-15; Gal. 1
11. ☐ Deut. 16-18; Ps. 38; Gal. 2
12. ☐ Deut. 19-21; Gal. 3
13. ☐ Deut. 22-24; Gal. 4
14. ☐ Deut. 25-27; Gal. 5
15. ☐ Deut. 28,29; Gal. 6
16. ☐ Deut. 30,31; Ps. 40; 1 Cor. 1
17. ☐ Deut. 32-34; 1 Cor. 2
18. ☐ Josh. 1,2; Ps. 37; 1 Cor. 3
19. ☐ Josh. 3-6; 1 Cor. 4
20. ☐ Josh. 7,8; Ps. 69; 1 Cor. 5
21. ☐ Josh. 9-11; 1 Cor. 6
22. ☐ Josh. 12-14; 1 Cor. 7
23. ☐ Josh. 15-17; 1 Cor. 8
24. ☐ Josh. 18-20; 1 Cor. 9
25. ☐ Josh. 21,22; Ps. 47; 1 Cor. 10
26. ☐ Josh. 23,24; Ps. 44; 1 Cor. 11
27. ☐ Judg. 1-3; 1 Cor. 12
28. ☐ Judg. 4,5; Ps. 39,41; 1 Cor. 13
29. ☐ Judg. 6,7; Ps. 52; 1 Cor. 14
30. ☐ Judg. 8; Ps. 42; 1 Cor. 15
31. ☐ Judg. 9,10; Ps. 49; 1 Cor. 16

WHEN READING THE BIBLE LOOK FOR:

What do I learn about God; about man?
Is there a sin to avoid; a command to obey?

WWW.DAILYTRANSFORMATION.ORG

Bible Reading Plan
THROUGH THE BIBLE IN ONE YEAR

READ THROUGH THE BIBLE ②

APRIL

1 ☐ Judg. 11,12; Ps. 50; 2 Cor. 1
2 ☐ Judg. 13-16; 2 Cor. 2
3 ☐ Judg. 17,18; Ps. 89; 2 Cor. 3
4 ☐ Judg. 19-21; 2 Cor. 4
5 ☐ Ruth 1,2; Ps. 53,61; 2 Cor. 5
6 ☐ Ruth 3,4; Ps. 64,65; 2 Cor. 6
7 ☐ 1 Sam. 1,2; Ps. 66; 2 Cor. 7
8 ☐ 1 Sam. 3-5; Ps. 77; 2 Cor. 8
9 ☐ 1 Sam. 6,7; Ps. 72; 2 Cor. 9
10 ☐ 1 Sam. 8-10; 2 Cor. 10
11 ☐ 1 Sam. 11,12; 1 Chr. 1; 2 Cor. 11
12 ☐ 1 Sam. 13; 1 Chr. 2,3; 2 Cor. 12
13 ☐ 1 Sam. 14; 1 Chr. 4; 2 Cor. 13
14 ☐ 1 Sam. 15,16; 1 Chr. 5; Mt. 1
15 ☐ 1 Sam. 17; Ps. 9; Mt. 2
16 ☐ 1 Sam. 18; 1 Chr. 6; Ps. 11; Mt. 3
17 ☐ 1 Sam. 19; 1 Chr. 7; Ps. 59; Mt. 4
18 ☐ 1 Sam. 20,21; Ps. 34; Mt. 5
19 ☐ 1 Sam. 22; Ps. 17,35; Mt. 6
20 ☐ 1 Sam. 23; Ps. 31,54; Mt. 7
21 ☐ 1 Sam. 24; 1 Chr. 8; Ps. 57,58; Mt. 8
22 ☐ 1 Sam. 25,26; Ps. 63; Mt. 9
23 ☐ 1 Sam. 27; 1 Chr. 9; Ps. 141; Mt. 10
24 ☐ 1 Sam. 28,29; Ps. 109; Mt. 11
25 ☐ 1 Sam. 30,31; 1 Chr. 10; Mt. 12
26 ☐ 2 Sam. 1; Ps. 140; Mt. 13
27 ☐ 2 Sam. 2; 1 Chr. 11; Ps. 142; Mt. 14
28 ☐ 2 Sam. 3; 1 Chr. 12; Mt. 15
29 ☐ 2 Sam. 4,5; Ps. 139; Mt. 16
30 ☐ 2 Sam. 6; 1 Chr. 13; Ps. 68; Mt. 17

MAY

1 ☐ 1 Chr. 14,15; Ps. 132; Mt. 18
2 ☐ 1 Chr. 16; Ps. 106; Mt. 19
3 ☐ 2 Sam. 7; 1 Chr. 17; Ps. 2; Mt. 20
4 ☐ 2 Sam. 8,9; 1 Chr. 18,19; Mt. 21
5 ☐ 2 Sam. 10; 1 Chr. 20; Ps. 20; Mt. 22
6 ☐ 2 Sam. 11,12; Ps. 51; Mt. 23
7 ☐ 2 Sam. 13,14; Mt. 24
8 ☐ 2 Sam. 15,16; Ps. 32; Mt. 25
9 ☐ 2 Sam. 17; Ps. 71; Mt. 26
10 ☐ 2 Sam. 18; Ps. 56; Mt. 27
11 ☐ 2 Sam. 19,20; Ps. 55; Mt. 28
12 ☐ 2 Sam. 21-23; 1 Th. 1
13 ☐ 2 Sam. 24; 1 Chr. 21; Ps. 30; 1 Th. 2
14 ☐ 1 Chr. 22-24; 1 Th. 3
15 ☐ 1 Chr. 25-27; 1 Th. 4

16 ☐ 1 Ki. 1; 1 Chr. 28; Ps. 91; 1 Th. 5
17 ☐ 1 Ki. 2; 1 Chr. 29; Ps. 95; 2 Th. 1
18 ☐ 1 Ki. 3; 2 Chr. 1; Ps. 78; 2 Th. 2
19 ☐ 1 Ki. 4,5; 2 Chr. 2; Ps. 101; 2 Th. 3
20 ☐ 1 Ki. 6; 2 Chr. 3; Ps. 97; Rom. 1
21 ☐ 1 Ki. 7; 2 Chr. 4; Ps. 98; Rom. 2
22 ☐ 1 Ki. 8; 2 Chr. 5; Ps. 99; Rom. 3
23 ☐ 2 Chr. 6,7; Ps. 135; Rom. 4
24 ☐ 1 Ki. 9; 2 Chr. 8; Ps. 136; Rom. 5
25 ☐ 1 Ki. 10,11; 2 Chr. 9; Rom. 6
26 ☐ Prov. 1-3; Rom. 7
27 ☐ Prov. 4-6; Rom. 8
28 ☐ Prov. 7-9; Rom. 9
29 ☐ Prov. 10-12; Rom. 10
30 ☐ Prov. 13-15; Rom. 11
31 ☐ Prov. 16-18; Rom. 12

JUNE

1 ☐ Prov. 19-21; Rom. 13
2 ☐ Prov. 22-24; Rom. 14
3 ☐ Prov. 25-27; Rom. 15
4 ☐ Prov. 28,29; Ps. 60; Rom. 16
5 ☐ Prov. 30,31; Ps. 33; Eph. 1
6 ☐ Ecc. 1-3; Ps. 45; Eph. 2
7 ☐ Ecc. 4-6; Ps. 18; Eph. 3
8 ☐ Ecc. 7-9; Eph. 4
9 ☐ Ecc. 10-12; Ps. 94; Eph. 5
10 ☐ Song 1-4; Eph. 6
11 ☐ Song 5-8; Phil. 1
12 ☐ 1 Ki. 12; 2 Chr. 10,11; Phil. 2
13 ☐ 1 Ki. 13,14; 2 Chr. 12; Phil. 3
14 ☐ 1 Ki. 15; 2 Chr. 13,14; Phil. 4
15 ☐ 1 Ki. 16; 2 Chr. 15,16; Col. 1
16 ☐ 1 Ki. 17-19; Col. 2
17 ☐ 1 Ki. 20,21; 2 Chr. 17; Col. 3
18 ☐ 1 Ki. 22; 2 Chr. 18,19; Col. 4
19 ☐ 2 Ki. 1-3; Ps. 82; 1 Tim. 1
20 ☐ 2 Ki. 4,5; Ps. 83; 1 Tim. 2
21 ☐ 2 Ki. 6,7; 2 Chr. 20; 1 Tim. 3
22 ☐ 2 Ki. 8,9; 2 Chr. 21; 1 Tim. 4
23 ☐ 2 Ki. 10; 2 Chr. 22,23; 1 Tim. 5
24 ☐ 2 Ki. 11,12; 2 Chr. 24; 1 Tim. 6
25 ☐ Joel 1-3; 2 Tim. 1
26 ☐ Jon. 1-4; 2 Tim. 2
27 ☐ 2 Ki. 13,14; 2 Chr. 25; 2 Tim. 3
28 ☐ Amos 1-3; Ps. 80; 2 Tim. 4
29 ☐ Amos 4-6; Ps. 86; Tit. 1
30 ☐ Amos 7-9; Ps. 104; Tit. 2

WHEN READING THE BIBLE LOOK FOR:

*What do I learn about God;
about man?
Is there a sin to avoid;
a command to obey?*

WWW.DAILYTRANSFORMATION.ORG

BiBle Reading Plan
THROUGH THE BIBLE IN ONE YEAR

• • • • • • • • • • • • • •

READ THROUGH THE BIBLE

③

JULY

1. ☐ Is. 1-3; Tit. 3
2. ☐ Is. 4,5; Ps. 115,116; Jude
3. ☐ Is. 6,7; 2 Chr. 26,27; Philemon
4. ☐ 2 Ki. 15,16; Hos. 1; Heb. 1
5. ☐ Hos. 2-5; Heb. 2
6. ☐ Hos. 6-9; Heb. 3
7. ☐ Hos. 10-12; Ps. 73; Heb. 4
8. ☐ Hos. 13,14; Ps. 100,102; Heb. 5
9. ☐ Mic. 1-4; Heb. 6
10. ☐ Mic. 5-7; Heb. 7
11. ☐ Is. 8-10; Heb. 8
12. ☐ Is. 11-14; Heb. 9
13. ☐ Is. 15-18; Heb. 10
14. ☐ Is. 19-21; Heb. 11
15. ☐ Is. 22-24; Heb. 12
16. ☐ Is. 25-28; Heb. 13
17. ☐ Is. 29-31; Jas. 1
18. ☐ Is. 32-35; Jas. 2
19. ☐ 2 Ki. 17; 2 Chr. 28; Ps. 46; Jas. 3
20. ☐ 2 Chr. 29-31; Jas. 4
21. ☐ 2 Ki. 18,19; 2 Chr. 32; Jas. 5
22. ☐ Is. 36,37; Ps. 76; 1 Pet. 1
23. ☐ 2 Ki. 20; Is. 38,39; Ps. 75; 1 Pet. 2
24. ☐ Is. 40-42; 1 Pet. 3
25. ☐ Is. 43-45; 1 Pet. 4
26. ☐ Is. 46-49; 1 Pet. 5
27. ☐ Is. 50-52; Ps. 92; 2 Pet. 1
28. ☐ Is. 53-56; 2 Pet. 2
29. ☐ Is. 57-59; Ps. 103; 2 Pet. 3
30. ☐ Is. 60-62; Jn. 1
31. ☐ Is. 63,64; Ps. 107; Jn. 2

AUGUST

1. ☐ Is. 65,66; Ps. 62; Jn. 3
2. ☐ 2 Ki. 21; 2 Chr. 33; Jn. 4
3. ☐ Nah. 1-3; Jn. 5
4. ☐ 2 Ki. 22; 2 Chr. 34; Jn. 6
5. ☐ 2 Ki. 23; 2 Chr. 35; Jn. 7
6. ☐ Hab. 1-3; Jn. 8
7. ☐ Zeph. 1-3; Jn. 9
8. ☐ Jer. 1,2; Jn. 10
9. ☐ Jer. 3,4; Jn. 11
10. ☐ Jer. 5,6; Jn. 12
11. ☐ Jer. 7-9; Jn. 13
12. ☐ Jer. 10-12; Jn. 14
13. ☐ Jer. 13-15; Jn. 15
14. ☐ Jer. 16,17; Ps. 96; Jn. 16
15. ☐ Jer. 18-20; Ps. 93; Jn. 17

16. ☐ 2 Ki. 24; Jer. 22; Ps. 112; Jn. 18 **③**
17. ☐ Jer. 23,25; Jn. 19
18. ☐ Jer. 26,35,36; Jn. 20
19. ☐ Jer. 45-47; Ps. 105; Jn. 21
20. ☐ Jer. 48,49; Ps. 67; 1 Jn. 1
21. ☐ Jer. 21,24,27; Ps. 118; 1 Jn. 2
22. ☐ Jer. 28-30; 1 Jn. 3
23. ☐ Jer. 31,32; 1 Jn. 4
24. ☐ Jer. 33,34; Ps. 74; 1 Jn. 5
25. ☐ Jer. 37-39; Ps. 79; 2 Jn.
26. ☐ Jer. 50,51; 3 Jn.
27. ☐ Jer. 52; Rev. 1; Ps. 143,144
28. ☐ Ezek. 1-3; Rev. 2
29. ☐ Ezek. 4-7; Rev. 3
30. ☐ Ezek. 8-11; Rev. 4
31. ☐ Ezek. 12-14; Rev. 5

SEPTEMBER

1. ☐ Ezek. 15,16; Ps. 70; Rev. 6
2. ☐ Ezek. 17-19; Rev. 7
3. ☐ Ezek. 20,21; Ps. 111; Rev. 8
4. ☐ Ezek. 22-24; Rev. 9
5. ☐ Ezek. 25-28; Rev. 10
6. ☐ Ezek. 29-32; Rev. 11
7. ☐ 2 Ki. 25; 2 Chr. 36; Jer. 40,41; Rev. 12
8. ☐ Jer. 42-44; Ps. 48; Rev. 13
9. ☐ Lam. 1,2; Obad.; Rev. 14
10. ☐ Lam. 3-5; Rev. 15
11. ☐ Dan. 1,2; Rev. 16
12. ☐ Dan. 3,4; Ps. 81; Rev. 17
13. ☐ Ezek. 33-35; Rev. 18
14. ☐ Ezek. 36,37; Ps. 110; Rev. 19
15. ☐ Ezek. 38,39; Ps. 145; Rev. 20
16. ☐ Ezek. 40,41; Ps. 128; Rev. 21
17. ☐ Ezek. 42-44; Rev. 22
18. ☐ Ezek. 45,46; Luke 1
19. ☐ Ezek. 47,48; Luke 2
20. ☐ Dan. 5,6; Ps. 130; Luke 3
21. ☐ Dan. 7,8; Ps. 137; Luke 4
22. ☐ Dan. 9,10; Ps. 123; Luke 5
23. ☐ Dan. 11,12; Luke 6
24. ☐ Ezra 1; Ps. 84,85; Luke 7
25. ☐ Ezra 2,3; Luke 8
26. ☐ Ezra 4; Ps. 113,127; Luke 9
27. ☐ Hag. 1,2; Ps. 129; Luke 10
28. ☐ Zech. 1-3; Luke 11
29. ☐ Zech. 4-6; Luke 12
30. ☐ Zech. 7-9; Luke 13

WHEN READING THE BIBLE LOOK FOR:

*What do I learn about God;
about man?
Is there a sin to avoid;
a command to obey?*

WWW.DAILYTRANSFORMATION.ORG

Bible Reading Plan
THROUGH THE BIBLE IN ONE YEAR

READ THROUGH THE BIBLE

④

OCTOBER

1. ☐ Zech. 10-12; Ps. 126; Luke 14
2. ☐ Zech. 13,14; Ps. 147; Luke 15
3. ☐ Ezra 5,6; Ps. 138; Luke 16
4. ☐ Est. 1,2; Ps. 150; Luke 17
5. ☐ Est. 3-8; Luke 18
6. ☐ Est. 9,10; Luke 19
7. ☐ Ezra 7,8; Luke 20
8. ☐ Ezra 9,10; Ps. 131; Luke 21
9. ☐ Neh. 1,2; Ps. 133; Luke 22
10. ☐ Neh. 3,4; Luke 23
11. ☐ Neh. 5,6; Ps. 146; Luke 24
12. ☐ Neh. 7,8; Acts 1
13. ☐ Neh. 9,10; Acts 2
14. ☐ Neh. 11,12; Ps. 1; Acts 3
15. ☐ Neh. 13; Mal. 1,2; Acts 4
16. ☐ Mal. 3,4; Ps. 148; Acts 5
17. ☐ Job 1,2; Acts 6,7
18. ☐ Job 3,4; Acts 8,9
19. ☐ Job 5; Ps. 108; Acts 10,11
20. ☐ Job 6-8; Acts 12
21. ☐ Job 9,10; Acts 13,14
22. ☐ Job 11,12; Acts 15,16
23. ☐ Job 13,14; Acts 17,18
24. ☐ Job 15; Acts 19,20
25. ☐ Job 16; Acts 21-23
26. ☐ Job 17; Acts 24-26
27. ☐ Job 18; Ps. 114; Acts 27,28
28. ☐ Job 19; Mark 1,2
29. ☐ Job 20; Mark 3,4
30. ☐ Job 21; Mark 5,6
31. ☐ Job 22; Mark 7,8

NOVEMBER

1. ☐ Ps. 121; Mark 9,10
2. ☐ Job 23,24; Mark 11,12
3. ☐ Job 25; Mark 13,14
4. ☐ Job 26,27; Mark 15,16
5. ☐ Job 28,29; Gal. 1,2
6. ☐ Job 30; Ps. 120; Gal. 3,4
7. ☐ Job 31,32; Gal. 5,6
8. ☐ Job 33; 1 Cor. 1-3
9. ☐ Job 34; 1 Cor. 4-6
10. ☐ Job 35,36; 1 Cor. 7-8
11. ☐ Ps. 122; 1 Cor. 9-11
12. ☐ Job 37,38; 1 Cor. 12
13. ☐ Job 39,40; 1 Cor. 13,14
14. ☐ Ps. 149; 1 Cor. 15,16
15. ☐ Job 41,42; 2 Cor. 1,2

16. ☐ 2 Cor. 3-6
17. ☐ 2 Cor. 7-10
18. ☐ Ps. 124; 2 Cor. 11-13
19. ☐ Mt. 1-4
20. ☐ Mt. 5-7
21. ☐ Mt. 8-10
22. ☐ Mt. 11-13
23. ☐ Mt. 14-16
24. ☐ Mt. 17-19
25. ☐ Mt. 20-22
26. ☐ Mt. 23-25
27. ☐ Ps. 125; Mt. 26,27
28. ☐ Mt. 28; 1 Th. 1-3
29. ☐ 1 Th. 4,5; 2 Th. 1-3
30. ☐ Rom. 1-4

DECEMBER

1. ☐ Rom. 5-8
2. ☐ Rom. 9-12
3. ☐ Rom. 13-16
4. ☐ Eph. 1-4
5. ☐ Eph. 5,6; Ps. 119:1-80
6. ☐ Phil. 1-4
7. ☐ Col. 1-4
8. ☐ 1 Tim. 1-4
9. ☐ 1 Tim. 5,6; Tit. 1-3
10. ☐ 2 Tim. 1-4
11. ☐ Philem. 1; Heb. 1-4
12. ☐ Heb. 5-8
13. ☐ Heb. 9-11
14. ☐ Heb. 12,13; Jude
15. ☐ Jas. 1-5
16. ☐ 1 Pet. 1-5
17. ☐ 2 Pet. 1-3; Jn. 1
18. ☐ Jn. 2-4
19. ☐ Jn. 5,6
20. ☐ Jn. 7,8
21. ☐ Jn. 9-11
22. ☐ Jn. 12-14
23. ☐ Jn. 15-18
24. ☐ Jn. 19-21
25. ☐ 1 Jn. 1-5
26. ☐ Ps. 117,119:81-176; 2 Jn.; 3 Jn.
27. ☐ Rev. 1-4
28. ☐ Rev. 5-9
29. ☐ Rev. 10-14
30. ☐ Rev. 15-18
31. ☐ Rev. 19-22

WHEN READING THE BIBLE LOOK FOR:

*What do I learn about God;
about man?
Is there a sin to avoid;
a command to obey?*

WWW.DAILYTRANSFORMATION.ORG

Fellowship

Fellowship: FINDING WEEKLY ENCOURAGEMENT

• • • • • • • • • • • • • • •

Jesus is concerned that we have loving unity with other Followers (John 17:21). It is His plan for us to grow (1 Thessalonians 5:11, Romans 12:10, Hebrews 3:13), support (Matthew 18:19-20) and care (Galatians 5:13, Colossians 3:12-13) for each other through life until we are home with Him. Healthy fellowship is a sign to the world that we are His followers (John 13:35).

A healthy Small Group regularly gathers for Bible Study living SAFER Values:

Shepherding Significant Caring (Acts 20:28)
Authority is the Bible (2 Timothy 3:16)
Fellowship We can know and be known, understood. (Acts 2:44-47)
Expansion We include those seeking to meet Jesus (Acts 2:47)
Reproduction A healthy place to make disciples as Jesus asks
(John 13:15, 2 Tim 2:2)

We can learn from the early church when they met regularly for Fellowship in Acts 2:36-47:

Baptism: *"Each of you must repent of your sins, turn to God, and be baptized in the name of Jesus Christ to show that you have received forgiveness for your sins. Then you will receive the gift of the Holy Spirit." (v38)*

Caring Leaders: *"They devoted themselves to the Apostle's..." (V42)*

God's Word: *"And with many other words he bore witness and continued to exhort them..." (V40) "They devoted themselves to the Apostle's teaching..." (V42)*

Love: *"...and fellowship..." (V42)*

Eating and Communion: *"...and to sharing in the Lord's Supper..." (V42)*

Prayer: *"...and in prayer..." (V42)*

Laying on of Hands: *"And awe came upon every soul, and many wonders and signs were being done through the apostles. (V43) (James 5:14)*

Giving: *"... They sold their possessions and shared the proceeds with those in need..." (V45)*

Worship: *"...praising God..." (V47)*

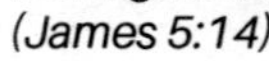

Make Disciples: *"...and having favor with all the people. And the Lord added to their number day by day those who were being saved." (V47)*

Fellowship: FINDING WEEKLY ENCOURAGEMENT

Share leadership:

Invite participants to share ownership of the group by giving them responsibilities. You can have a host responsible for asking people to help bring food and to set up, a prayer leader can keep the prayer list with answers and a worship leader can choose songs for the group to sing. Another person can organize the group to care through work projects. God has distributed spiritual gifts among the members. So, let them use their gifts! Remember: the ultimate goal is for each group member to become a trainer like you and start their own group! *(See page 122 and follow the QR codes for video instruction.)*

How to conduct a meeting:

This model is called Three-thirds: 3/3. There are three parts to a meeting and plan that each part takes equal time. (I.E. 120 minute meeting, reserve 40 minutes for each part).

 **Looking Back**    **Looking Up**   **Looking Ahead** »

« Part 1: Looking Back

You can share a meal while you: a) care for group members; b) worship by singing a song; c) being accountable by checking their growth at following Jesus and fishing for men; and, d) vision casting by examining the health of your group compared to the 10 things in Acts 2:36-47.

Part 2: Looking Up

This is your lesson time. A simple and effective way to help people get into the Bible is to work through a book chapter by chapter. Consider studying for your first 11 weeks the following Bible passages : *1) Repent/Believe - Luke 19:1-10; 2) Be Baptized - Acts 8:26-39; 3) Pray - Matthew 6:5-15; 4) Make Disciples - John 4:4-42; 5) Bible Study - 2 Timothy 3:1-17; 6) Love - Luke 10:25-37 7) Lord's Supper - Luke 22:7-20; 8) Give - Mark 12:41-44; 9) Church - Acts 2:36-47; 10) Supernatural Power - John 15:1-27, note Matthew 10:7-8 and James 5:14-15; and 11) Persevere - Acts 5:27-42.* When done, move to the gospel of Mark. When studying a passage it is helpful to ask and answer the following 4 questions as a group (Take notes on the following Weekly Fellowship Meeting pages. One page for each week):

FELLOWSHIP: FINDING WEEKLY ENCOURAGEMENT

Warm Up Question: Which verse spoke to me the most and why? Did another verse create questions?

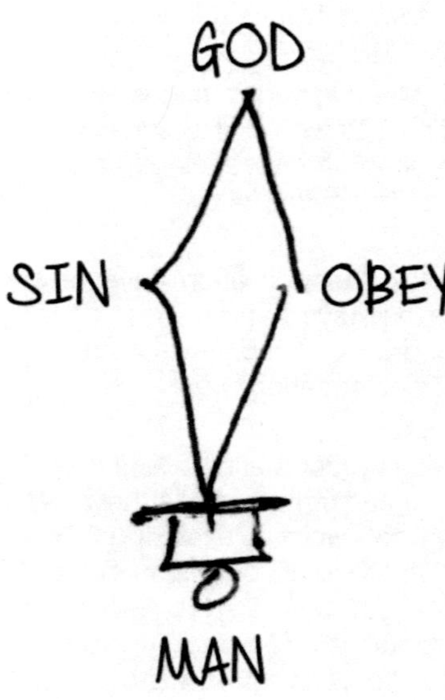

1) What did you learn about **God?**

2) What did you learn about **man?**

3) Is there a **sin** to avoid?

4) Is there a command to **obey?**

Application Question: How does God want me to apply what I just learned?

Note: Since our new identity is to make disciples, ask, "With who can I share the truth I've *learned?*"

» Part 3: Looking Ahead

a) Have members practice teaching the lesson you just modeled with pairs or have one or two practice (depending on time available) with the whole group.
b) Second, spend time praying and listening to God about how He would have them obey. Have members share what their goal is. At the next meeting during the accountability time willing participants can share a story of their progress.

• • • • • • • • • • • • • • • •

How to Use the DT Journal in Your Home Group Meeting

Disciple making begins as group members practice the "Four Things." Below is noted the discipline and the week you would implement it.

Using the weekly Fellowship Meeting Pages (pages 123-135), you will have 11 commands of Jesus as your next 11 weeks of lessons. At the bottom of page 119, the lessons and their Bible study scripture passages are listed in the Looking Up section. You can incorporate the "Four Things" as follows:

- **LISTEN** (Prayer) on week 3. For application, have the group review the Listening primer (Page 4) and use the Prayers and Answer log (pages 5-8). Each week add to the prayer log as your group takes prayer requests. For additional help see video: "Listen" at DailyTransformation.Org.

- **INQUIRE** (Daily Bible Reading/Journaling): Jesus says we need more than bread to eat. We need spiritual bread from God (Matthew 4:4). On week 5 we learn the importance of studying God's word by exploring 2 Timothy 3:1-17. For your application, Turn to the SOAP method of Journaling (pages 10-13) and note the LIFE Journal Reading Plan (Pages 113-116). Note today's New Testament reading and let your group do a 15 minute exercise so they can write their first journal entry and Table of Content notation. For help, the group could watch: "Inquire" video at DailyTransformation.Org.

- **FELLOWSHIP** (Weekly Group Bible Study): In week 9 the group will look at the importance of the church in Acts 2:36-47. Note the 10 traits of a healthy group (page 119). In the Looking Ahead portion, ask the group to evaluate its health. What can our group work on to be healthier? The weekly Looking Back section will invite you to do the same evaluation each week. This is a good time to ask your group members if they have started a group for those they have been sharing Jesus with. Encourage them to look at their OIKOS map (pages 138-139) and ask their friends if one of them would host and start a meeting in the next week. For additional help see: "Fellowship" video at DailyTransformation.Org.

- **EXPRESS** (Sharing Jesus): Week 4 you will learn about making disciples reading John 4:4-42. In the Looking Ahead portion of your meeting, turn to page 137 and have each person write their 90 second testimony. Pair up to practice. Each week, have one share during the Looking Back time. Have a part two to this topic the following week and train the members in the Three Circles (pages 138-139). Help? See videos: "Express 1 and 2" at DailyTransformation.Org.

Invite your friends to journal and fellowship with you in Bible study. Download the Daily Transformation Journal for free from Google Play or from the Apple Store.

DailyTransformation.Org

Weekly Fellowship Meeting Pages

Coaching to Lead a Fellowship Group
12-Minute Videos

WEEK 0	WEEK 1	WEEK 2

WEEK 3	WEEK 4	WEEK 5

WEEK 6	WEEK 7	WEEK 8

WEEK 9	WEEK 10	WEEK 11

⟪ LOOKING BACK:

Share how I applied last week's goal, something from my daily inquire journaling using SOAP or a God story from this past week:

Express: Someone practice their Jesus story (testimony)

Group Vision: Which of the 10 traits should our group focus on to become healthier?

⌃ LOOKING UP:

(After reading the passage of study, have one person recount it in his own words.) Which verse spoke the most to me and why? Does another verse create questions?

What did I learn about God?

What did I learn about man?

Is there a sin to avoid?

A command to obey?

⟫ LOOKING AHEAD:

What is God asking me to do?

Who do I need to share this truth with?

Prayer: Share and pray for members' needs adding requests to "Prayers & Answers" pages 5-8.

《 LOOKING BACK:

Share how I applied last week's goal, something from my daily inquire journaling using SOAP or a God story from this past week:

Express: Someone practice their Jesus story (testimony)

Group Vision: Which of the 10 traits should our group focus on to become healthier?

《 LOOKING UP:

(After reading the passage of study, have one person recount it in his own words.) Which verse spoke the most to me and why? Does another verse create questions?

What did I learn about God?

What did I learn about man?

Is there a sin to avoid?

A command to obey?

》 LOOKING AHEAD:

What is God asking me to do?

Who do I need to share this truth with?

Prayer: Share and pray for members' needs adding requests to "Prayers & Answers" pages 5-8.

⟪ LOOKING BACK:

Share how I applied last week's goal, something from my daily inquire journaling using SOAP or a God story from this past week:

Express: Someone practice their Jesus story (testimony)

Group Vision: Which of the 10 traits should our group focus on to become healthier?

⌃ LOOKING UP:

(After reading the passage of study, have one person recount it in his own words.) Which verse spoke the most to me and why? Does another verse create questions?

What did I learn about God?

What did I learn about man?

Is there a sin to avoid?

A command to obey?

⟫ LOOKING AHEAD:

What is God asking me to do?

Who do I need to share this truth with?

Prayer: Share and pray for members' needs adding requests to "Prayers & Answers" pages 5-8.

❮❮ LOOKING BACK:

Share how I applied last week's goal, something from my daily inquire journaling using SOAP or a God story from this past week:

Express: Someone practice their Jesus story (testimony)

Group Vision: Which of the 10 traits should our group focus on to become healthier?

⌃⌃ LOOKING UP:

(After reading the passage of study, have one person recount it in his own words.) Which verse spoke the most to me and why? Does another verse create questions?

What did I learn about God?

What did I learn about man?

Is there a sin to avoid?

A command to obey?

❯❯ LOOKING AHEAD:

What is God asking me to do?

Who do I need to share this truth with?

Prayer: Share and pray for members' needs adding requests to "Prayers & Answers" pages 5-8.

《 LOOKING BACK:

Share how I applied last week's goal, something from my daily inquire journaling using SOAP or a God story from this past week:

Express: Someone practice their Jesus story (testimony)

Group Vision: Which of the 10 traits should our group focus on to become healthier?

⌃ LOOKING UP:

(After reading the passage of study, have one person recount it in his own words.) Which verse spoke the most to me and why? Does another verse create questions?

What did I learn about God?

What did I learn about man?

Is there a sin to avoid?

A command to obey?

》 LOOKING AHEAD:

What is God asking me to do?

Who do I need to share this truth with?

Prayer: Share and pray for members' needs adding requests to "Prayers & Answers" pages 5-8.

◀◀ LOOKING BACK:

Share how I applied last week's goal, something from my daily inquire journaling using SOAP or a God story from this past week:

Express: Someone practice their Jesus story (testimony)

Group Vision: Which of the 10 traits should our group focus on to become healthier?

▲▲ LOOKING UP:

(After reading the passage of study, have one person recount it in his own words.) Which verse spoke the most to me and why? Does another verse create questions?

What did I learn about God?

What did I learn about man?

Is there a sin to avoid?

A command to obey?

▶▶ LOOKING AHEAD:

What is God asking me to do?

Who do I need to share this truth with?

Prayer: Share and pray for members' needs adding requests to "Prayers & Answers" pages 5-8.

❮❮ LOOKING BACK:

Share how I applied last week's goal, something from my daily inquire journaling using SOAP or a God story from this past week:

Express: Someone practice their Jesus story (testimony)

Group Vision: Which of the 10 traits should our group focus on to become healthier?

❮❮ LOOKING UP:

(After reading the passage of study, have one person recount it in his own words.) Which verse spoke the most to me and why? Does another verse create questions?

What did I learn about God?

What did I learn about man?

Is there a sin to avoid?

A command to obey?

❯❯ LOOKING AHEAD:

What is God asking me to do?

Who do I need to share this truth with?

Prayer: Share and pray for members' needs adding requests to "Prayers & Answers" pages 5-8.

《 LOOKING BACK:

Share how I applied last week's goal, something from my daily inquire journaling using SOAP or a God story from this past week:

Express: Someone practice their Jesus story (testimony)

Group Vision: Which of the 10 traits should our group focus on to become healthier?

《 LOOKING UP:

(After reading the passage of study, have one person recount it in his own words.) Which verse spoke the most to me and why? Does another verse create questions?

What did I learn about God?

What did I learn about man?

Is there a sin to avoid?

A command to obey?

》 LOOKING AHEAD:

What is God asking me to do?

Who do I need to share this truth with?

Prayer: Share and pray for members' needs adding requests to "Prayers & Answers" pages 5-8.

⟪ LOOKING BACK:

Share how I applied last week's goal, something from my daily inquire journaling using SOAP or a God story from this past week:

Express: Someone practice their Jesus story (testimony)

Group Vision: Which of the 10 traits should our group focus on to become healthier?

⟰ LOOKING UP:

(After reading the passage of study, have one person recount it in his own words.) Which verse spoke the most to me and why? Does another verse create questions?

What did I learn about God?

What did I learn about man?

Is there a sin to avoid?

A command to obey?

⟫ LOOKING AHEAD:

What is God asking me to do?

Who do I need to share this truth with?

Prayer: Share and pray for members' needs adding requests to "Prayers & Answers" pages 5-8.

❮❮ LOOKING BACK:

Share how I applied last week's goal, something from my daily inquire journaling using SOAP or a God story from this past week:

Express: Someone practice their Jesus story (testimony)

Group Vision: Which of the 10 traits should our group focus on to become healthier?

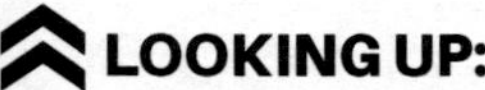

❮❮ LOOKING UP:

(After reading the passage of study, have one person recount it in his own words.) Which verse spoke the most to me and why? Does another verse create questions?

What did I learn about God?

What did I learn about man?

Is there a sin to avoid?

A command to obey?

❯❯ LOOKING AHEAD:

What is God asking me to do?

Who do I need to share this truth with?

Prayer: Share and pray for members' needs adding requests to "Prayers & Answers" pages 5-8.

⟪ LOOKING BACK:

Share how I applied last week's goal, something from my daily inquire journaling using SOAP or a God story from this past week:

Express: Someone practice their Jesus story (testimony)

Group Vision: Which of the 10 traits should our group focus on to become healthier?

⟰ LOOKING UP:

(After reading the passage of study, have one person recount it in his own words.) Which verse spoke the most to me and why? Does another verse create questions?

What did I learn about God?

What did I learn about man?

Is there a sin to avoid?

A command to obey?

⟫ LOOKING AHEAD:

What is God asking me to do?

Who do I need to share this truth with?

Prayer: Share and pray for members' needs adding requests to "Prayers & Answers" pages 5-8.

⟪ LOOKING BACK:

Share how I applied last week's goal, something from my daily inquire journaling using SOAP or a God story from this past week:

Express: Someone practice their Jesus story (testimony)

Group Vision: Which of the 10 traits should our group focus on to become healthier?

⌃ LOOKING UP:

(After reading the passage of study, have one person recount it in his own words.) Which verse spoke the most to me and why? Does another verse create questions?

What did I learn about God?

What did I learn about man?

Is there a sin to avoid?

A command to obey?

⟫ LOOKING AHEAD:

What is God asking me to do?

Who do I need to share this truth with?

Prayer: Share and pray for members' needs adding requests to "Prayers & Answers" pages 5-8.

≪ LOOKING BACK:

Share how I applied last week's goal, something from my daily inquire journaling using SOAP or a God story from this past week:

Express: Someone practice their Jesus story (testimony)

Group Vision: Which of the 10 traits should our group focus on to become healthier?

⌃ LOOKING UP:

(After reading the passage of study, have one person recount it in his own words.) Which verse spoke the most to me and why? Does another verse create questions?

What did I learn about God?

What did I learn about man?

Is there a sin to avoid?

A command to obey?

≫ LOOKING AHEAD:

What is God asking me to do?

Who do I need to share this truth with?

Prayer: Share and pray for members' needs adding requests to "Prayers & Answers" pages 5-8.

express

EXPRESS: *Sharing God's Love*

• • • • • • • • • • • • • •

When you discover and stay close to the truth of your need for God's grace each day, your passion to share this hope with others stays hot! Jesus wants to be your first love and then wants you to share Him with others.

"For God was in Christ, reconciling the world to Himself, no longer counting people's sins against them. This is the wonderful message He has given us to tell others. We are Christ's ambassadors, and God is using us to speak to you." **2 Corinthians 5:19-21 (NLT)**

TWO PARTS OF CHRIST'S MESSAGE

Scan and watch video for additional help

The Unique Part: Your Story
The story of how I began a relationship with Jesus. Two examples:

- **King David:** *"Come and listen…and I will tell you what He did for me."* Psalm 66:16 (NLT)

- **The Woman at the Well:** *"Many Samaritans from the village believed in Jesus because the woman had said, 'He told me everything I ever did!'"* John 4:39 (NLT)

Your story is a 90-second explanation of your journey with Jesus. Do not focus on stories, but a few words that describe your life (For example: *broken, hurting, confused, Does God care?*). It is important to hear from your acquaintance. Follow your share with a caring question like, *"Have you discovered Jesus loves you too?"* Polish and practice telling your story by recording it on your phone. Consider posting your video or sharing it with your friends.

« Describe what your life was like before Jesus and any awareness of your need for

Him. ____

____

⌃ How did you commit your life to Jesus? ___________________________

____

____

» Describe how Jesus answered your pain and concerns. ___________________

____

____

Care Question: ____

EXPRESS: SHARING GOD'S LOVE

The Universal Part: The Good News
Explaining how someone can become a follower of Jesus Christ.

a. Three Circles. Ask your friend for a piece of paper so you can draw them a picture. You will give it to them when you're done.

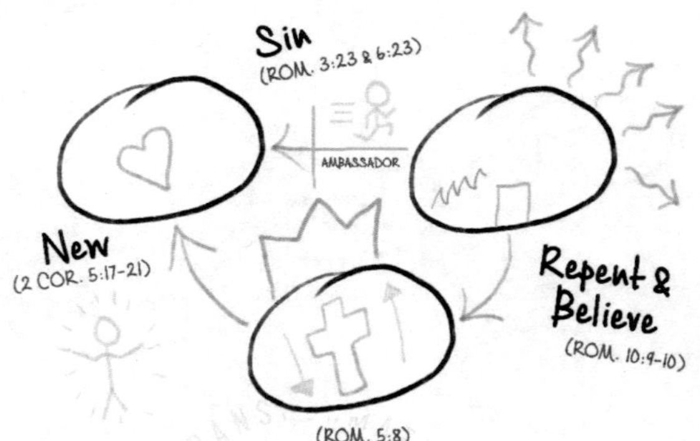

Scan and watch video for additional help

1) Draw first circle with a crack. This represents our broken world. Disease, disasters, broken relationships. Each squiggly line represents our attempt to feel better (Job, Family, Drugs, Sex). But, nothing lasts.

2) Draw second circle with a heart. This was God's plan for us. God designed the world as a place to be in relationship with us. We can know He loves and forgives us. Nature is a beautiful gift demonstrating His love. But, Sin (draw a vertical line) keeps us from experiencing God's plan.

3) Draw the third circle with a cross in the middle. God loves us and wants to restore our relationship with Him. He came to earth as Jesus (down arrow), died on the cross and on the third day rose (up arrow) as He promised. Restoration and forgiveness requires us to make Jesus King of our life (drawn crown). How do we make Him King? We must "Repent and Believe" (draw words) (Romans 10:9,10). Draw picture of a person kneeling.

4) Ask the person which of the two top circles they are currently experiencing? Brokenness or Sensing God's love? Invite them to pray so they can turn from self-leadership to God's and to turn from sin to God's plan. (Pray ABC: ADMIT-I Sin, forgive me; BELIEVE-I believe you, Jesus, are God and died to pay for my sins; CONFESS- I make you my God.)

5) Share with them their new identity: 2 Corinthians 5:17-21 says they are a new creation (draw picture with radiant lines around the person). It also says they are an ambassador for Jesus to help their family and friends (Oikos) move from brokenness to forgiveness, too. (Draw stick figure running on line between God's Plan and Brokenness).

6) Invite them to a Bible study with you to learn more.

7) Draw a circle and invite them to identify and write down their five closest family & friends (Oikos) who they need to share this drawing. (sample on next page)

EXPRESS: *Sharing God's Love*

● ● ● ● ● ● ● ● ● ● ● ● ●

Sample Oikos circle. Place your name in the center circle and identify 5 people close to you who need to hear about Jesus and place their names in the outer circles.

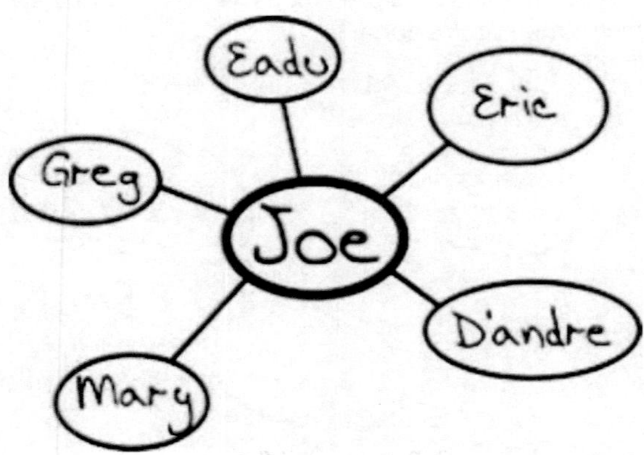

b. The Romans Road is a way to show a person their need and how to repent that they may choose to follow Jesus. (You can mark your Bible with a page number of the next verse to quickly find it. The first reference (Romans 3:23, page________) would be written just inside the front cover.

- **Romans 3:23 (All Have Sinned)** *"For everyone has sinned; we all fall short of God's glorious standard."*

- **Romans 6:23 (Sin's Penalty)** *"For the wages of sin is death, but the free gift of God is eternal life through Christ Jesus our Lord."*

- **Romans 5:8 (Christ Paid the Penalty)** *"But God showed his great love for us by sending Christ to die for us while we were still sinners."*

- **Romans 10:9,10 (Salvation through Faith)** *"If you confess with your mouth that Jesus is Lord and believe in your heart that God raised him from the dead, you will be saved. For it is by believing in your heart that you are made right with God, and it is by confessing with your mouth that you are saved."*

Sharing List: On the next page we have provided a place for you to write down the names of those with whom you are sharing Jesus. We recommend you begin with those relationally closest to you (Oikos: Greek for household). Who in your world are you concerned they do not have peace with God? Make a list. Pray and ask God to prepare their hearts to hear. Write in the date you first shared. When you discover they have surrendered their life to Jesus, write in that salvation date and when they were baptized. Finally, train them to faithfully follow Jesus by practicing together the My LIFE Journal. Please note when you start.

EXPRESS: Sharing God's Love

PERSON	SHARED	ACCEPTS	BAPTISM	L.I.F.E.

EXPRESS: *Sharing God's Love*

PERSON		SHARED	ACCEPTS	BAPTISM	L.I.F.E.

USING A COMP BOOK FOR
DAILY TRANSFORMATION JOURNAL

• • • • • • • • • • • • •

Create your own Daily Transformation LIFE journal
with a composition book or spiral notebook.
The following instructions will help you!

Start on Page 1:
- Title the top of the page **Listen to God Through Prayer**.
- Create three columns labeled **Date**, **Prayer Request**, and **Answer Date**.
- Leave three pages total set aside for your prayer request list.

Listen to God Through Prayer

Date	Prayer Request	Answer Date

Go to Page 4:
- Title the top of the page **Inquire God of His Will through Bible Reading and Journaling**.
- Add below the title **Table of Contents**.
- Create four columns labeled **Date**, **Bible Verse**, **Title**, and **Page**.
- Leave six pages total set aside for the Table of Contents.

Inquire God of His Will through Bible Reading and Journaling
Table of Contents

Date	Bible Verse	Title	Page
4/23	Matthew 10:27	Hope to share	1
4/24	Psalm 109:21	God protects me from my enemies	2
4/25	1 Chronicles 10:13	Earthly consequences for my sin	3

Go to Page 10:
This is the first of your **Daily Bible Reading Journal** pages.

Now go to the back of the journal:
- Count back two pages (single sheet of paper).
- Title the top of this second to last page **Express What Jesus is Doing in My Life**.
- Create five columns labeled **Name**, **Date Shared**, **Date Accepts Jesus**, **Date Baptized**, **Date Trained in LIFE**.

Express What Jesus is Doing in My Life

Name	Date Shared	Date Accepts Jesus	Date Baptized	Date Trained in LIFE

Count back 20 more pages (10 sheets) and title the top of the page **Fellowship Bible Study With Friends.**

Create three sections down the page with the following questions.

I. Looking Back:
How have you applied last weeks goal? Who will practice their 90-second testimony? Which church circle characteristic should we work on?

II. Looking Up:
Someone give a summary of the passage just read. Answer the following five questions:

1) Which verse spoke the most to you and why or which created questions for you?

2) What do you learn about **God**?

3) What do you learn about **man**?

4) Is there a **sin** to avoid?

5) Is there a command to **obey?**

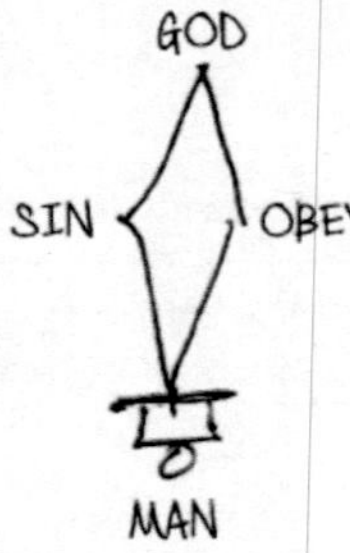

III. Looking Ahead:
Ask, 6) What is God asking you to do?

7) Who can you share this passage with? Record prayer requests from the group praying for the needs and help applying what you learned.

Use the same method for thirteen Fellowship Meetings.

Invite your friends to journal and fellowship with you in Bible study. Download the Daily Transformation Journal for free.

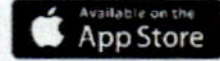

DailyTransformation.Org

SPIRITUAL GROWTH *survey*

• • • • • • • • • • • • • •

Name ____

Email ____

Phone ____

I'm taking this assessment on: ______/______/______ (today's date and choose one):

- ☐ The day of My Life Journal commitment
- ☐ After 1 month of My Life Journal
- ☐ After 90 days of My Life Journal
- ☐ My 1 year anniversary

In the past month...

How many times did you attend worship service? *(circle one)* **0 1 2 3 4+**

How intimate would you say your prayer time is with God? **1** *(cold)*-**10** *(life-giving)* ______

How often did you read your Bible in a week? *(circle one)* **0 1 2 3 4 5 6 7**

Is journaling on your Bible reading a normal habit? *(circle one)* **Y   N**

How often did you meet with a small group for Bible study and fellowship? *(circle one)*

0 1 2 3 4+

How many people did you share the Gospel with? *(circle one)* **0 1 2 3 4 5 6 7 8 9 10+**

How would the following 14 markers describe your life? 1 *(not much)* - **10** *(definitely)*

1. I desire to know God in a deeper way. (Phil. 3:7-11; Ps. 42:1; 63:1) ______

2. I receive God's truth with joy even though it's hard and I suffer. (Acts 14:22) ______

3. I serve God because I want to see Him glorified. (Col. 3:17; 1 Cor. 10:31) ______

4. I meet intimately with God as I pray and read my Bible. (1 Pet. 2:1; Col. 2:6-7; 4:2; Heb. 4:16) ______

5. I am growing in my understanding of the Bible and doctrine. (2 Pet. 3:16; Heb. 5:11-14) ______

6. I have loving community with Christians and serve them. (1 Thess. 5:11; 1 John 4:7) ______

7. I live out my faith as I relate to my family. (Col. 3:18-21) ______

8. I share Jesus' grace, love and truth with my family, neighbors, and world. (Col. 4:3-6) ______

9. I fight to control my struggles with sin. (Col. 3:5) ______

10. Those close to me say I am maturing into the image of Jesus. (Gal. 5:22-23) ______

11. The Holy Spirit is enabling me to serve and reveal Jesus' Kingdom. (Luke 10:9; Acts 1:8) ______

12. People are choosing to follow Jesus after I share Him and His Gospel. (Acts 2:41) ______

13. I am starting Bible study groups for those I share Christ. (Heb. 10:24-25) ______

14. I am training others to share Jesus and to start their own groups. (Pro. 14:4; Acts 14:21-23) ______

Please give this survey to your trainer or email to survey@dailytransformation.org

ABOUT THE AUTHOR

• • • • • • • • • • • • • • •

Dr. David Carothers is a second generation Nevadan and met Jesus at Camp Lee Canyon in 1976. Christ set David on course to train him to trust and obey Him. God called David into ministry while attending Pepperdine University where he earned a BS in Business. The first place David would follow Christ was to the inner-city of Philadelphia where he worked with students. There he met a young lady from Iowa who was serving Jesus in a private Christian school. Together they served, leading teens to be disciples of Jesus. In 1992, David and Joan were married and served in David's home church in Las Vegas as a Singles Pastor. After the internship they moved to Fort Worth, Texas for David to attend Southwestern Baptist Theological Seminary where he earned a Master of Divinity (MDiv) and helped start Discovery Church. In 1996, they moved to northern California to join Twin Cities Church, a church plant in their fourth year. Their daughter Abigail was born the same year followed by Andrew, Aaron, and Amara. In 2010, God led David to serve in a church in central California, where they served for 8 years. He was a very active pastor, serving in the larger community on several non-profit boards and raising the value of prayer in the community.

In 2018, David and his family relocated to his home city of Las Vegas and founded Daily Transformation which has begun work on several continents. Their focus is helping seekers, scattered sheep, stuck sheep, and shepherds have a LIFE-transforming relationship with Jesus. The Daily Transformation Journal in your hands has been translated into more than a dozen languages and is available on your smartphone. These four habits are proven tools helping people across cultural and geographical boundaries. In June 2001, Pastor Wayne Cordeiro taught David the second habit, the Bible Reading Plan and SOAP journaling method. The third habit, Fellowship, is a compilation of the Discovery Bible Study Method adapted in the mission field by No Place Left and DT's ongoing global work. The fourth habit, Express, employs the three-circle method developed by missionaries and modified to establish the Bible's authority when sharing Why Jesus Died.

In late 2020, Daily Transformation began First Love Bible College to train pastors and Christian leaders in Christian theology at no cost to the student. Today they have sites in several countries including Pakistan, Uganda, and USA. David has continued his education, earning a Master of Theology (ThM) and Doctor of Ministry (DMin) focusing on church revitalization. David not only pastors in the local church but helps pastors and their churches experience revitalization by working on Jesus as First Love and bearing First Things fruit of sharing Christ and developing reproducing disciples of Jesus.